Parrots, poets, philosophers, & good advice

Raymond Geuss

Hearing Eye
1999

Published by
Hearing Eye
Box 1
99 Torriano Avenue
London NW5 2RX

This publication has been made possible with
the financial assistance of the London Arts Board.

Printed by Aldgate Press, London E1

Typeset by
Daniel James at Copyart, London NW5

ISBN 1 870841 63 8

ἄλλους <μέν> τινας ἔφη ὁ Ἀριστόδημος οἴχεσθαι ἀπιόντας, ἓ δὲ ὕπνον
λαβεῖν, καὶ καταδαρθεῖν πάνυ πολύ... ἐξεγρέσθαι δὲ πρὸς ἡμέραν ἤδη
ἀλεκτρυόνων ᾀδόντων, ἐξεγρόμενος δὲ ἰδεῖν τοὺς μὲν ἄλλους καθεύδοντας
καὶ οἰχομένους, Ἀγάθωνα δὲ καὶ Ἀριστοφάνη καὶ Σωκράτη ἔτι μόνους
ἐγρηγορέναι καὶ πίνειν ἐκ φιάλης μεγάλης ἐπὶ δεξιά. τὸν οὖν Σωκράτη
αὐτοῖς διαλέγεσθαι... <καὶ> προσαναγκάζειν τὸν Σωκράτη ὁμολογεῖν
αὐτοὺς τοῦ αὐτοῦ ἀνδρὸς εἶναι κωμῳδίαν καὶ τραγῳδίαν ἐπίστασθαι ποιεῖν,
καὶ τὸν τέχνῃ τραγῳδοποιὸν ὄντα καὶ κωμῳδοποιὸν εἶναι.

(Plato *Symposium* 223)

Eventually I passed out, and when I came to again I saw that it was just
before dawn and everyone else was either sleeping it off or had gone home.
All that is, except Agathon, Aristophanes, and Sokrates. They were still
swigging out of a large jar they were passing around, with Sokrates gabbing
at the others as usual, trying to force them to agree that anyone who *really*
knew how to write tragedies would also *have to* know how to write
comedies, 'and vice versa'.

Index

Introduction

This is a series of didactic poems devoted to instructing the reader how to live. This genre has recently, i.e. during the past two hundred years or so, fallen into desuetude, but deserves revival. The collection treats many of the traditional topics of this kind of poetry: eating and drinking, the characteristic difficulties encountered in various professions, indigency, old age, personal appearance and hygiene, sexual aberration, the posthumous evaluation of human achievement etc.

Some of the poems stand in a distinct relation to certain antecedents from the corpus of ancient literature. Few are anything like direct translations, and even those that may at first glance have this appearance, will on closer inspection be found to be marred (or embellished, depending on the reader's taste) by deviations. To facilitate comparison the publisher has kindly allowed me to include the antecedent poems. In one case (poem 5) I originally wrote in German, then in English; the English version appeared in *London Review of Books* (December 12, 1996). I have included both versions. Ten of the other poems appeared in *Translation and Literature* (University of Edinburgh Press, autumn 1998).

The Greek or Latin text used is, unless otherwise indicated, in each case the most recent one to appear in the *Oxford Classical Texts* series. The newly rediscovered epigrams of Marcus Marulus Spalatensis have been edited by Darko Novakovic and published in *Colloquia Maruliana* VI ed. B. Lucin and M.Tomasovic (Split: Knjizevni Krug Split 1997).

I use the following abbreviations:

AP for *Anthologia Palatina* ed. Jacobs (Leipzig, 1814)
EP for *Epigrammata Graeca* ed. D.L. Page (Oxford, 1975)
LG for *Lyra Graeca Selecta* ed. D.L. Page (Oxford, 1968)
CIL for *Corpus Inscriptionum Latinarum*

My thanks to Hilary Gaskin, Richard Rorty, and Quentin Skinner for much good advice, not all of which, however, I have followed.

Raymond Geuss

Cui dono?

To whom will I give this spanking new
volume of libels, slanders, and *sottises*,
neatly printed and spiffily bound?
Pista, to you, who taught me
to read Nestroy and turn *Catull*
into Hapsburg-German (of a kind),
because you always told the truth
and said my nothings were just nothing.
Enjoy this book in hell. Light up a fag,
flirt with the Irish waitresses
down there, and rest content:
Your teaching has paid off.

Speechless

PARROT, Prince among birds, delightful slave,
you speak just like a person, and make more sense
than most, repeating to us what we say to you.
Who closed off your pipes so suddenly?
Just yesterday you were an honoured guest
at dinner and we watched you flit about
from couch to couch, plucking dainties
from the table-tops until well after midnight;
anyone who spoke to you, received a civil answer.
All the while, you perched at death's door. Now
you've feathered off for good into oblivion.

Cui dono lepidum nouum libellum
arida modo pumice expolitum?
Corneli, tibi: namque tu solebas
meas esse aliquid putare nugas
iam tum, cum ausus es unus Italorum
omne aeuum tribus explicare cartis
doctis, Iuppiter, et laboriosis.
quare habe tibi quidquid hoc libelli
qualecumque; quod, <o> patrona virgo,
plus uno maneat perenne saeclo.

Catullus, I

Psittace, dux uolucrum, domini facunda uoluptas
humanae sollers imitator psittace linguae,
quis tua tam subito praeclusit murmura fato?
hesternas, miserande, dapes moriturus inisti
nobiscum, et gratae carpentem munera mensae
errantemque toris mediae plus tempore noctis
uidimus. adfatus etiam meditataque uerba
reddideras. at nunc aeterna silentia Lethes
ille canorus habes.

Statius, Silvae, II.4

Mercenaries

Rations

My spear is my meat and drink,
and when I drink,
it props me up.

The unceasing glorious struggle
to hellenize Macedonia

I've just made some Shiptar's day:
he has the shield I threw away
I saved my skin, so what do I care;
shields, after all, can be replaced.

Après

'Special Auxiliary Forces' are welcome,
Franz, for just as long as the fighting lasts.

Fides

Trust your brother (if he's still alive);
trust your neighbour if he's at your side.
Trust the mercenary
if he's standing right up front
with your spear-point near his back.

I

ἐν δορὶ μέν μοι μᾶζα μεμαγμένη, ἐν δορὶ δ᾽ οἶνος
Ἰσμαρισκός, πίνω δ ᾽ἐν δορὶ κεκλιμένος.

II

ἀσπίδι μὲν Σαΐων τις ἀγάλλεται, ἣν παρὰ θάμνῳ
ἔντος ἀμώμητον κάλλιπον οὐκ ἐθέλων,
αὐτὸν δ᾽ ἐξεσάωσα. τί μοι μέλει ἀσπὶς ἐκείνη;
ἐρρέτω. ἐξαῦτις κτήσομαι οὐ κακίω.

III

Γλαῦκ᾽ ἐπίκουρος ἀνὴρ τόσσον φίλος ἔστε μάχηται.

Archilochos, 2,5,*15 (ed. West)

11

A.D. 14

The comedy begins like this: (1)
'In my nineteenth year
on my own authority   (2)
I raised an army
to drive into exile
the murderers of my father'   (3)
(well, actually my great-uncle).
'On my own authority'
means I started a civil war.

'Bloodthirsty little boy' he called me,   (4)
that vain chatterbox, who hoped
to use me for his own ends,
'a young man to be praised, fêted,
(then done away with)'   (5)
but he got me wrong. I wasn't
usable. *'Either fuck me or fight':*
the choice Fulvia offered was really
no choice at all. *'My prick is dearer to me*
than my life; let the trumpets sound.'   (6)
Agrippa and I made short work
of barking Anubis.   (7)

'As victor I spared the lives
of all citizens who asked
for mercy'. (Mr Mouth   (8)
hadn't been the kind
to ask for mercy) *'In my sixth*
and seventh consulships
I handed over the republic
from my control to the discretion
of the Senate and the Roman People.'   (9)
My best joke of all. Who
would have thought
no one would laugh
for 600 years?

1. *'Comoedia finita est'* (Suetonius, *Vita diui Augusti*)

2. *'Annos undeuiginti natus exercitum priuato consilio comparaui'*
   (Res gestae diui Augusti I.1)

3. *'Qui parentem meum trucidauerunt, eos in exilium expulsi'*
   (Res gestae diui Augusti II.1)

4. *'adulescentulus carnifex'* {actually used of Pompey}

5. *'laudandum adulescentem, ornandum, tollendum'*
   (Cicero, Ad Familiares XI.20)

6. *'Fuluiam ego ut futuam? quod si me Manius oret*
   pedicem, faciam? non puto, si sapiam,
   "aut futue, aut pugnemus" ait. quid quod mihi uita
   carior est ipsa mentula? signa canant!'
   (Martial XI.20)

7. *'latrator Anubis'* *(Virgil, Aeneid VIII.698)*

8. *'uictorque omnibus ueniam petentibus ciuibus peperci'*
   (Res gestae diui Augusti III.1)

9. *'In consulatu sexto et septimo, rem publicam ex mea potestate in*
   senatus populusque Romani arbitrium transtuli.'
   (Res gestae diui Augusti XXXIV.1)

Noli admirari

No wonder, Rufus,
no girlie
will spread her thighs for you
unless you bribe her
with expensive clothes, jewellery, etc.
The reason is the bad press
you have: People say
a he-goat lives in your armpits.
Offputting that,
distinctly offputting.
No chippie likes to bed down
in a barnyard.
Call off your indecent assault
on our noses
or stop being surprised
when the popsies give you the pass.

Kein Wunder, Rufus, daß Dir keine
die Schenkel spreizt, es sei denn
Du stimmst sie um mit Bargeld.
Es geht, mein Freund,
ein bös' Gerücht um: Ein Ziegenbock,
heißt es, hat Obdach jetzt gefunden
unter Deinem Hemd. Abstoßend, gelt?
Einem saubren Mädchen kommt so was
natürlich nicht ins Haus.
Verjage nun das penetrante Tier,
das uns die Luft verpestet
oder hör' auf zu maulen, wenn
die Flittchen Dich umgehn.

Noli admirari, quare tibi femina nulla,
Rufe, uelit tenerum supposuisse femur,
non si illam rarae labefactes munere uestis
aut perluciduli deliciis lapidis.
laedit te quaedam mala fabula, qua tibi fertur
ualle sub alarum trux habitare caper.
hunc metuunt omnes, neque mirum: nam mala ualde est
bestia, nec quicum bella puella cubet.
quare aut crudelem nasorum interfice pestem,
aut admirari desine cur fugiunt.

Catullus, LXIX

Urbs

Lucius Tarquinius

    (known to Romans

        as 'Tarquinius Priscus')

first Etruscan king

    was also an

        early reformer

who is credited with

    constructing the

        Cloaca Maxima

which slopes away from

    the Esquiline

        down to the Tiber.

Later politicians

    have usually

        tended to reverse this.

Anacreonta

I.

The dry earth drinks up rain.
Californians drink in the sun.
Plants and animals drink.
It seems to be
a law of nature.
So why bother me?

II.

Women say: 'Raymond,
look at yourself;
you've got no hair.'

'Geriatric case, or not,
I need it. It makes sense
for old men to tank up
before the long haul.'

Pets

Wicked cat, bad as a pack of dogs,
why did you bite the head
off Master's budgie?
Meanwhile the mice cavort
about the house
and gnaw our bones.

I

ἡ γῆ μέλαινα πίνει,
πίνει δὲ δένδρε᾽ αὖ γῆν.
πίνει θάλασσ᾽ ἀναύρος
ὁ δ᾽ ἥλιον θάλασσαν.
τὸν δ᾽ ἥλιον σελήνη.
τί μοι μάχεσθ᾽, ἑταῖροι,
καὐτῶι θέλοντι πίνειν;

II

λέγουσιν αἱ γυναῖκες·
᾽Ανάκρεον, γέρων εἶ,
λαβὼν ἔσοπτρον ἄθρει
κόμας μὲν οὐκέτι οὔσας,
ψιλὸν δέ σευ μέτωπον.᾽
ἐγὼ δὲ τὰς κόμας μέν,
εἴτ᾽ εἰσὶν εἴτ᾽ ἀπῆλθον,
οὐκ οἶδα. τοῦτο δ᾽ οἶδα,
ὡς τῶι γέροντι μᾶλλον
πρέπει τὸ τέρπνα παίζειν
ὅσωι πέλας τὰ Μοίρης.

Carmina anacreontea 21 & 7 (ed. West, Leipzig 1993)

ἀνδροβόρων ὁμότεχνε κυνῶν, αἴλουρε κακίστη,
τῶν ᾽Ακταιονίδων ἐσσὶ μία σκυλάκων,
κτήτορος ᾽Αγαθίαο τεοῦ πέρδικα φαγοῦσα,
λυπεῖς, ὡς αὐτὸν κτήτορα δασσαμένη.
καὶ σὺ μὲν ἐν πέρδιξιν ἔχεις νόον. οἱ δὲ μύες νῦν
ὀρχοῦνται, τῆς σῆς δραξάμενοι σπατάλης.

Damocharis *AP* VII.206

17

Epitaphs

I

Wine, hot baths, sex:
the steepest road to hell.

II

Shouting 'Farewell, Sun',
Nigel jumped off a high wall:
read too much Plato.

III

Diodoros had sailed the blue: Gibraltar,
Cyprus, Egypt, everywhere. To celebrate
his safe return, he held an on-board feast.
The food and drink were copious,
indeed excessive. While barfing he
slipped off the prow, the harbour-water
barely deep enough to drown him

IV

Think of Euboulos
abstemious as they come
dead now all the same.

I

οἶνος καὶ τὰ λοετρὰ καὶ ἡ περὶ Κύπριν ἐρωή
ὀξυτέρην πέμπει τὴν ὁδὸν εἰς Ἀίδην.

Anonymous, AP X.112

II

εἴπας ΄ Ἥλιε, χαῖρε· Κλεόμβροτος ὠμβρακιώτης
    ἥλατ΄ ἀφ΄ ὑψηλοῦ τείχεος εἰς Ἀίδην,
ἄξιον οὐδὲν ἰδὼν θανάτου κακόν, ἀλλὰ Πλάτωνος
    ἓν τὸ περὶ ψυχῆς γράμμ΄ ἀναλεξάμενος.

Kallimachos, EG LIII

III

εἰδότα κἠπ΄ Ἄτλαντα τεμεῖν πόρον, εἰδότα Κρήτης
    κύματα καὶ πόντου ναυτιλίην μέλανος,
Καλλιγένευς Διόδωρον Ὀλύνθιον ἴσθι θανόντα
    ἐν λιμένι, πρῴρης νύκτερον ἐκχύμενον,
δαιτὸς ἐκεῖ τὸ περισσὸν ὅτ΄ ἤμεεν. ἇ πόσον ὕδωρ
    ὤλεσε τὸν τόσσῳ κεκριμένον πελάγει.

Antipater of Sidon, AP VII..625

IV

μεμνῆσθ΄ Εὐβούλοιο σαόφρονος ὦ παριόντες
    πίνωμεν. κοινὸς πᾶσι λιμὴν Ἀίδης.

Leonidas of Tarentum, AP VII.452

A father's wisdom

We all avoid a stinker, son,
so mind your manners well:
In the theatre
don't hiss the actors
everybody likes. When out
to dinner never blow
your nose on the table cloth
– one of your fellow-guests
might be fastidious.
If you meet ladies
in the street, refrain
from dropping your drawers
to show your private parts
(unless you've been already
introduced). Remember, too:
A man who has just lost
a case in court, may not
be in the mood for jokes,
and never *ever* make it known
to all and sundry in a barber shop
that you intend to drink that night.

Cenabis bene

You'll dine well at my place, Fabullus,
if you bring all the food. (I can
give you a list.) My wallet's
full of cobwebs at the moment;
my company is all I can provide.
Plus one other little thing,
which, when you smell it,
will make you wish you were all nose.

ὁ δὲ βδελυρὸς τοιοῦτός τις οἷος
ἀπαντήσας γυναιξὶν ἐλευθέραις
ἀνασυράμενος δεῖξαι τὸ αἰδοῖον
καὶ ἐν θεάτρῳ συρίττειν οὓς ἡδέως
θεωροῦσιν οἱ λοιποὶ
καὶ ἡττωμένῳ δὲ μεγάλην δίκην
ἀπιόντι ἀπὸ τοῦ δικαστηρίου
προσελθεῖν καὶ συνησθῆναι
καὶ διηγεῖσθαι προσστὰς πρὸς κουρεῖον
ἢ μυροπώλιον ὅτι μεθύσκεσθαι μέλλει.

Theophrastus, *Characteres* XI

Cenabis bene, mi Fabulle, apud me
paucis, si tibi di fauent, diebus,
si tecum attuleris bonam atque magnam
cenam, non sine candida puella
et uino et sale et omnibus cachinnis.
haec si, inquam, attuleris, uenuste noster,
cenabis bene; nam tui Catulli
plenus sacculus est aranearum.
sed contra accipies meros amores
seu quid suauius elegantiusue est:
nam unguentum dabo, quod meae puellae
donarunt Veneres Cupidinesque.
quod tu cum olfacies, deos rogabis,
totum ut te faciant, Fabulle, nasum.

Catullus, XIII

Garlic

No Homer to be sure,
but he would *eat* anything.
When at the end of dinner–
spaghetti aglio e olio
(heavy on the aglio)–
seeking inspiration he began
'The Invocation of the Muses'
they decamped, driven off
by a ripe eructation.
Fortifying himself
with another, even heartier
helping of the main course,
he tried again. To no avail:
poetry and garlic don't mix.

Coniunx

Your wife once doted
on you. Why, you ask,
does she now give you
nought but grief?
'*Kvetch, kvetch, kvetch*'
all day. The change
is not surprising. She loved
the young stud
you once were;
an agèd codger
(with flaccid todger)
is much less to her taste.
If you want peace
when your beard is grey,
you've only one course:
emigration.

In Pamphagum malum poetam

Alia cenarat cupiens cum pangere uersus
  Pamphagus Aonias iussit adesse deas.
ast illae offensae diro ructantis odore
  conuersis capiunt passibus inde fugam.
lautius hinc pransus tentat reuocare fugaces
  sed neque sic pranso Pieris ulla fauet.
mitte aliis igitur condendi carmina curam:
  tu tantum uentrem, Pamphage, pasce tuum.

Marcus Marulus Spalatensis, 2

Quaeris cur coniunx, quae te dilexerat olim
  nunc fugit et duris litibus exagitat?
uerius haud possum quicquam tibi dicere, Marce:
  dilexit iuuenem, nunc fugit illa senem.
omnibus hoc uitium est miseros odisse maritos,
  aetas longa quibus languida membra facit.
uis tu pace frui, cum sit tibi candida barba,
  i procul atque alio uiuere disce loco.

Marcus Marulus Spalatensis, 4

23

Illusions

Someone told me of your end,
Herakleitos, and tears came
as I remembered how often we two
had outlasted the sun, talking,
and sunk him. Now you're long since
dead and decomposing somewhere,
old friend from Bodrum.
Still, your works will survive.*

       They haven't.

Nota

Why, when so many people
censure me because of what
I write, does this never happen
to my critics?

       Those who write
nothing are naturally immune.

Just visiting

Mice, if you're looking for food,
depart in peace: We're starving
ourselves. (Try next-door.)
If, however, you intend
to sharpen your teeth
on my papyrus rolls again,
you'll find you've come
to the wrong dinner-party.

εἶπέ τις, Ἡράκλειτε, τεὸν μόρον, ἐς δέ με δάκρυ
ἤγαγεν, ἐμνήσθην δ᾽ ὁσσάκις ἀμφότεροι
ἠέλιον λέσχῃ κατεδύσαμεν ἀλλὰ σὺ μέν που
ξεῖν᾽ Ἁλικαρνησεῦ, τετράπαλαι σποδίη.
αἱ δὲ τεαὶ ζώουσιν ἀηδόνες, ᾗσιν ὁ πάντων
ἁρπακτὴς Ἀΐδης οὐκ ἐπὶ χεῖρα βαλεῖ.

Kallimachos, EG XXXIV

Cur mea scripta notant multi, tua, critice, nemo?
unc qui nil scribit, critice, nemo notat.

Marcus Marulus Spalatensis, 26

ὦ μύες, εἰ μὲν ἐπ᾽ ἄρτον ἐληλύθατ᾽, ἐς μυχὸν ἄλλον
στείχετ᾽ – ἐπεὶ λιτὴν οἰκέομεν καλύβην –
οὗ καὶ πίονα τυρὸν ἀποδρέψεσθε καὶ αὔην
ἰσχάδα καὶ δεῖπνον συχνὸν ἀπὸ σκυβάλων.
εἰ δ᾽ ἐν ἐμαῖς βύβλοισι πάλιν καταθήξετ᾽ ὀδόντα,
κλαύσεσθ᾽, οὐκ ἀγαθὸν κῶμον ἐπερχόμενοι.

Ariston, EG III

Lust etc.

I

Nossie says: 'Sex beats
anything else for sweetness,
hands down. Compared
to it, I'd spit out even honey.
Anyone Venus hasn't snogged
wouldn't know a rose
from a rattle-snake.'

II

Two sharp pains, ooh! aah!
poverty, lust together.
Hunger I can stand.

III

What is on offer,
rose-girl? your roses? yourself?
or both together?

IV

When you swear you never do it for free,
I believe you. How much do you usually pay?

V

Jig-a-jig's super
but when, then, she asks for dosh
Ugh! bad medicine.

I

ἅδιον οὐδὲν ἔρωτος. ἃ δ᾽ ὄλβια, δεύτερα πάντα
ἐστίν. ἀπὸ στόματος δ᾽ ἔπτυσα καὶ τὸ μέλι.
τοῦτο λέγει Νοσσίς. τίνα δ᾽ ἁ Κύπρις οὐκ ἐφίλασεν
οὐκ οἶδεν τῆνας τἄνθεα, ποῖα ῥόδα.

Nossis, *EG* I

II

Paupertas me saeua domat dirusque Cupido:
sed toleranda fames, non tolerandus amor.

Esuriens pauper telis incendor Amoris.
inter utrumque malum, deligo pauperiem.

Claudius Claudianus, *Ep.* XXXIX & XL

III

ἡ τὰ ῥόδα, ῥοδόεσσαν ἔχεις χάριν. ἀλλὰ τί πωλεῖς;
σαυτήν, ἢ τὰ ῥόδα; ἠὲ συναμφότερα;

Dionysios, *EG* VI

IV

Lesbia se jurat gratis numquam esse fututam.
uerum est. cum futui uult, numerare solet.

Martial, XI.62

V

ἁδὺ τὸ βινεῖν ἐστί, τίς οὐ λέγει; ἀλλ᾽ ὅταν αἰτῇ
χαλκόν, πικρότερον γίνεται ἐλλεβόρου.

Killaktor, *AP* V.29

Glubit

That Lesbia,
Caelius, you remember,
the one we both enjoyed.
the one who turned my head,
you know her latest trick?
In alleys and dark corners
she plays at glub-glub
with the randy sons of Remus.

Lost lines from <u>Aeneid</u> VI

And I saw Catullus wandering there *distrait*
among the shades, and murmuring to himself:
glupsitne? glupsitne? glupsitne?

Zoe

Zoe keeps a tame,
bearded grammarian
at home to help her
practice her declensions
and (best of all)
conjugations.

Timon

When the misanthrope died they asked:
'Well, Tom, satisfied now?'
'No, indeed' he replied,
'there are even more of you here in hell.'

Caeli, Lesbia nostra, Lesbia illa,
illa Lesbia, quam Catullus unam
plus quam se atque suos amauit omnes,
nunc in quadriuiis et angiportis
glubit magnanimi Remi nepotes.

Catullus LVIII

γραμματικὸν Ζηνωνὶς ἔχει πώγωνα Μένανδρον,
   τὸν δ᾽ υἱον τούτῳ φησιν συνεστακέναι.
τὰς νύκτας δ᾽ αὐτῇ μελετῶν οὐ παύεται οὗτος
   πτώσεις, συνδέσμους, σχήματα, συζυγίας.

Lucillius *AP* XI.139

Τίμων, οὐ γὰρ ἔτ᾽ ἐσσί, τί τοι, σκότος ἢ φάος, ἐχθρόν;
   – τὸ σκότος, ὑμέων γὰρ πλείονες εἰν Ἀίδῃ.

Kallimachos, *EG* LI

29

Nicole

Some say, Nicole, you dye your hair,
but clearly you haven't touched it
since you bought it.

Medicus

When he was a surgeon he'd say
he'd 'operate';
now he calls himself
an 'undertaker'.
Change of names,
same profession.

A gambler

Why you lose?
You think
you know
what you don't.

Advice

Stranger, take good advice from a Sicilian:
Never go out drunk on a winter's night.

Action at a distance

The famous surgeon Pheidon
didn't operate; he didn't even
examine me. Just thinking
of his name killed me.

τὰς τρίχας, ὦ Νίκυλλα, τινὲς βάπτειν σε λέγουσιν
ἃς σὺ μελαινοτάτας ἐξ ἀγορᾶς ἐπρίω.

Lucillius, *AP* XI.68

Nuper erat medicus, nunc est uispillo Diaulus:
quod uispillo facit, fecerat et medicus.

Martial, I.47

Quolibet in ludo scis quare, Barthole, perdis?
hoc te quod nescis, Barthole, scire putas.

Marcus Marulus Spalatensis, 130

ξεῖνε, Συρακόσιός τοι ἀνὴρ τόδ᾽ ἐφίεται Ὄρθων·
χειμερίας μεθύων μηδαμὰ νυκτὸς ἴοις.

Theokritos, *EG* XII

οὔτ᾽ ἔκλυσεν Φείδων μ᾽ οὔθ᾽ ἥψατο. ἀλλὰ πυρέξας
ἐμνήσθην αὐτοῦ τοὔνομα, κἀπέθανον.

Nikarchos *AP* XI.118

31

Carol

I

Two came to Carol early in the day,
each wanting to go first, but Carol,
clever girl, was on top form:
One spread her legs in front;
the other hiked her skirt up in the back.

II

Why, Carol, were you taken
off to hell so suddenly?
You were only half as old as
Methuselah, but twice as
loud. You could still drown out
the whole slave-market
all by yourself or shout down
any pimp in town. May the earth
rest lightly upon you,
so the dogs have no trouble
digging you up.

Peditum

You claim to be my best friend,
but I see no evidence of this:
when I need money,
you refuse to lend it;
you've never yet invited me to dine;
I can't remember when you last
did me a favour or helped me out..
Your friendliness amounts to this:
you fart when I'm around
without restraint.

Cum duo uenissent ad Phyllida mane fututum
  et nudam cuperet sumere uterque prior,
promisit pariter se Phyllis utrique daturam,
  et dedit; ille pedem sustulit, hic tunicam.

Martial X.81

Saecula Nestoreae permensa, Philaeni, senectae
  rapta es ad infernas tam cito Ditis aquas?
Euboicae nondum numerabas longa sibyllae
  tempora: maior erat mensibus illa tribus.
Heu quae lingua silet! non illam mille catastae
  uincebant, nec quae turba Sarapin amat,
nec matutini cirrata caterua magistri,
  nec quae Strymonio de grege ripa sonat.
quae nunc Thessalico lunam deducere rhombo,
  quae sciet hos illos uendere lena toros?
sit tibi terra leuis mollique tegaris harena,
  ne tua non possint eruere ossa canes.

Martial IX.29

Cedere de nostris nulli te dicis amicis.
  sed, sit ut hoc uerum,quid ,rogo, Crispe, facis?
mutua cum peterem sestertia quinque, negasti,
  non caperet nummos cum grauis arca tuos.
quando fabae nobis modium farrisue dedisti,
  cum tua Niliacus rura colonus aret?
quando breuis gelidae missa est toga tempore brumae?
  argenti uenit quando selibra mihi?
nil aliud uideo quo te credamus amicum
  quam quod me coram pedere, Crispe, soles.

Martial X.15

33

More epitaphs

I

The men buried here
beat the Sicilians
fair and square
eight times in a row.

(The ninth time,
due to factors
beyond their control,
they lost.)

II

Celts need not apply

We three, well brought up, young
Hellenic ladies from Miletus,
lie here, dead by our own hands.
We couldn't stand the thought
of being forced to wed
insalubrious wild men in kilts,
to the wheeze of the bagpipes.

III

Pentheus got his bride Penthesilea,
but the wedding-banquet was not
a success. Twenty-four
guests dead; all buried here.

IV

Falling backwards from a little ladder,
this baby broke its tiny neck,
but, when it saw its master,
it stretched out its arms to him.
Dust, don't weigh down the bones
of this slave child.

οἵδε Συρακοσίους ὀκτὼ νίκας ἐκράτησαν
ἄνδρες, ὅτ᾽ ἦν τὰ θεῶν ἐξ ἴσου ἀμφοτέροις.

Euripides, *EG* II

οἰχόμεθ᾽, ὦ Μίλητε, φίλη πατρί, τῶν ἀθεμίστων
    τὴν ἄνομον Γαλατῶν ὕβριν ἀναινόμεναι,
παρθενικαὶ τρισσαὶ πολιήτιδες, ἃς ὁ βιατάς
    Κελτῶν εἰς ταύτην μοῖραν ἔτρεψεν Ἄρης.
οὐ γὰρ ἐμείναμεν ἄμμα τὸ δυσσεβὲς οὐδ᾽ Ὑμέναιον
    νυμφίον, ἀλλ᾽ Ἀΐδην κηδεμόν᾽ εὑρόμεθα.

Anyte, *EG* XXII

ἥρπασέ τις νύμφην, καὶ τὸν γάμον ἥρπασε δαίμων,
    ψυχῶν συλήσας τερπομένην ἀγέλην.
εἷς γάμος εἰκοσιπέντε τάφους ἔπλησε θανόντων.
    πάνδημος δὲ νεκρῶν εἷς γέγονεν θάλαμος.
νύμφη Πενθεσίλεια πολύστονε, νυμφίε Πενθεῦ,
    ἀμφοτέρων ὁ γάμος πλούσιος ἐν θανάτοις.

Palladas, *AP* VII.610

κλίμακος ἐξ ὀλίγης ὀλίγον βρέφος ἐν Διοδώρου
    κάππεσεν, ἐκ δ᾽ ἐάγη καίριον ἀστράγαλον
δινηθεὶς προκάρηνος. ἐπεὶ δ᾽ ἴδε θεῖον ἄνακτα
    ἀντόμενον, παιδνὰς αὐτίκ᾽ ἔτεινε χέρας.
ἀλλὰ σὺ νηπιάχου δμωός, κόνι, μήποτε βρίθειν
    ὀστέα, τοῦ διετοῦς φειδομένη Κόρακος.

Diodoros, *AP* VII.632

35

Youth and age

I

Still unyielding, she says she couldn't love
a one-eyed cannibal. No matter.
I'll keep on trotting down the mountain
to that sandy beach, humming to myself,
and won't stop asking her,
until the final spasm of senility.

II

People are so prejudiced.
On the *Corso Umberto*
no one ever greets me;
not even Madame Sahara
will give me the time of day.
Conversation stops dead
when I enter the café.
Fortunately the tourists like
my playing. It is true
that I am big and strong,
still have a booming voice,
and prefer my own company.
It is also, of course, true
that I can't see, but that's not
my fault and the rumors
about me are lies. Fabrications.
Transparent attempts
by those burglars I surprized
at home to shift attention
from themselves and what they did –
robbery and mutilation –
to me. Now if I didn't have
my musical career, I don't know
what would become of me.

αὐτὰρ ἐγὼν βασεῦμαι ἐμὰν ὁδὸν ἐς τὸ κάταντες
τῆνο ποτὶ ψαμαθόν τε καὶ αἰόνα ψιθυρίσδων
λισσόμενος Γαλάτειαν ἀπηνέα. τὰς δὲ γλυκείας
ἐλπίδας ὑστατίω μέχρι γήραος οὐκ ἀπολειψῶ.

Bion, XVI

Tempting

The pig gazed
at the proffered food
with interest,
but a glance
at the Minister's face
made him draw back,
full of mistrust.

Scholastikos

Scholastikos is a philosopher.
He reads books all day long.
In the morning he reads mathematical books,
in the afternoon metaphysical books;
at night it's political books.
One day he will write a book
on agriculture.

Trentotto

Are you worried, Cerinthus,
because I have a fever?
I certainly hope you are.
Otherwise I wouldn't recover;
what would be the point?

Toga

Many thanks, Cerinthus;
now I won't be surprised
or make a bad mistake.
Some, though,
might take it amiss
if I am supplanted
by a little seamstress.

Disappointed

I've come here in the middle of the night,
stealing away from my husband, drenched
by the rain; aren't you going to *do* anything?

Rumor

Rumor has it she's been misbehaving
(frequently). Now I wish I had no ears.
What doesn't pain me is no crime.
It's the sharp tongues that hurt. Quiet there!

Estne tibi, Cerinthe, tuae pia cura puellae,
quod mea nunc uexat corpora fessa calor?
a ego non aliter tristis euincere morbos.
optarim quam te si quoque uelle putem.
at mihi quid prosit morbos euincere, si tu
nostra potes lento pectore ferre mala?

Sulpicia, *Tibulli liber* III.18

Gratum est, securus multum quod iam tibi de me
permittis, subito ne male inepta cadam.
sit tibi cura togae potior pressumque quasillo
scortum quam Serui filia Sulpicia:
solliciti sunt pro nobis, quibus illa dolori est
ne cedam ignoto maxima causa toro.

Sulpicia, *Tibulli liber* III.17

καὶ νύκτος μεσάτης τὸν ἐμὸν κλέψασα σύνευνον
ἦλθον καὶ πυκινῇ τεγγομένη ψακάδι.
τοὔνεκ ἐν ἀπρήκτοισι καθήμεθα, κοὐχὶ λαλεῦντες
εὕδομεν ὡς εὕδειν τοῖς φιλέουσι θέμις;

Philodemos *AP* V. 120

Rumor ait crebro nostram peccare puellam:
nunc ego me surdis auribus esse uelim.
crimina non haec sunt nostra sine facta dolore:
quid miserum torques, rumor acerbe? tace.

Tibulli liber III.20

Graffiti

I

Darling, let's
pretend. This bed
will be a field,
and I'll be
your horsey.

II

Blondes
spoil my taste
for brunettes.

Fortunately
the effect
doesn't last.

Apophoreta

Andalusian girl

She twitches her thighs so enticingly she
would make even Saint Joseph jerk off.

Slave-Boy

Take home as a present from me
this toy-boy, so smooth and fresh,
you'll never look at a girl again.

Mea vita, meae deliciae,
ludamus parumper:
hunc lectum campum,
me tibi equom esse putamus.

Graffito from Pompei

Candida me docuit nigras odisse puellas
odero si potero si non inuitus amabo.

CIL, IV. 9847

Puella Gaditana

Tam tremulum crisat, tam blandum prurit, ut ipum
  masturbatorem fecerit Hippolytum.

Puer

Sit nobis aetate puer, non pumice leuis,
  propter quem placeat nulla puella mihi.

Martial XIV. 203 & 205

41

Klutaimnestra on Agamemnon

I stab him twice and twice he groans,
then buckles. When he's down
I give him one more for the road
to hell. At last I got what I had
wanted for so long, his corpse. He fell
and coughed his life out; as he did,
he showered me with sprays of blood,
all bright and lovely as the morning dew.
It gave me goose-flesh, but I
was proud and glad and loved it
more than when I lay in labour
and brought forth a child.

On a statue of Priapus

I priapize anyone I catch stealing from this garden:
the Pope, the Spice Girls, Mother Theresa.
even Moses himself; I'm no respecter of persons
You may think it isn't right to make such a fuss
for the sake of a few pumpkins, but it is; I say so.

Adonis in hell

Now that I'm here,
what from the world above
do I most regret?
The radiant disc
of the sun, the expanse
of stars on a cloudless
night, the calm visage
of the moon; also
cucumbers in season,
green, firm and juicy.

παίω δέ νιν δίς, κἀν δυοῖν οἰμωγμάτοιν
μεθῆκεν αὐτοῦ κῶλα, καὶ πεπτωκότι
τρίτην ἐπενδίδωμι, τοῦ κατὰ χθονός,
"Αιδου, νεκρῶν σωτῆρος, εὐκταίαν χάριν.
οὕτω τὸν αὐτοῦ θυμὸν ὁρμαίνει πεσών,
κἀκφυσιῶν ὀξεῖαν αἵματος σφαγὴν
βάλλει μ᾽ ἐρεμνῇ ψακάδι φοινίας δρόσου,
χαίρουσαν οὐδὲν ἧσσον ἢ διοσδότῳ
γάνει σπορητὸς κάλυκος ἐν λοχεύμασιν.

Aeschylus, *Agamemnon* 1384ff.

πάντα πριηπίζω, κἂν ᾖ Κρόνος. οὐ διακρίνω
   οὐδένα φῶρ᾽ οὕτω ταῖσδε παρὰ πρασιαῖς.
ἔπρεπε μὴ λαχάνων <ἕνεκεν> τάδε καὶ κολοκυνθῶν
   φήσει τις, με λέγειν. ἔπρεπεν, ἀλλὰ λέγω.

Tymnes, *EG* VII

κάλλιστον μὲν ἐγὼ λείπω φάος ἠελίοιο
δεύτερον ἄστρα φαεινὰ σεληναίης τε πρόσωπον
ἠδὲ καὶ ὡραίους σικύους καὶ μῆλα καὶ ὄγχνας.

Praxilla, *LG* 417

Gold medal

OK, you can run faster
than any man in town;
so can an ostrich.
You can jump farther,
so can a kangaroo.
As for your prodigious
ability to lift weights,
consider the jackass...

A natural mistake

Baby Jill can hardly talk:
'black' she'll say for white
and 'day' for night. She even
calls her mummie's husband 'da'.

Too late, though

Alive, this man was a slave.
Now he's the equal of any king.

If only

If only I were a warm spring breeze
you'd bare your breasts,
and clutch me, panting, to you.

Cinna

Cinna pretends to be poor
    and he is.

In Periclem bona corporis sui iactantem

Attollit nimium te gloria uana, Pericles,
  quod celeri excurris plana per arua pede,
quodque palestritis luctandi uiribus obstas,
  lumine quod sano quaeque minuta uides,
arrectaque leues quod colligis aure susurros,
  nescit odor nares quod latuisse tuas.
cursu te superant tygres, te uiribus ursi,
  plus oculis lynces, plus ualet aure lepus.
quam tibi odorandi canibus uis insita maior:
  naribus agnoscunt quo fera torsit iter.
quid te igitur magnum censes, insane Pericles,
  gloria quum pecudum non sit habenda minor?

Marcus Marulus Spalatensis, 4

De Ila seruo patre nata

Aethiopes cignos, nanos uocat Ila Cyclopas.
  non miror dominum si uocet illa patrem.

Marcus Marulus Spalatensis, 58

Μάνης οὗτος ἀνὴρ ἦν ζῶν ποτε, νῦν δὲ τεθνηκώς
  ἶσον Δαρείῳ τῷ μεγάλῳ δύναται.

Anyte, *EG* XXIII

εἴθ᾽ ἄνεμος γενόμην, σὺ δὲ δὴ στείχουσα παρ᾽ αὐγάς
  στήθεα γυμνώσαις καί με πνέοντα λάβοις

Anonymus, *EG* LXXII

Pauper uideri Cinna uult; et est pauper.

Martial, VIII.19

45

Biljoe

I

Biljoe is like a Spaniard,
he cleans his teeth with piss.
No wonder people are suspicious
when he shows off his smile.

II

Reading Martial

You're a con-man *(fraudator)*,
a thug *(lanista)*, and a stool-pigeon *(delator)*.
What's more
you like to suck cock *(fellator)*.
Are you *sure*
your name isn't
Biljoe?

III

A viper bit Biljoe
and he died
of blood poisoning.
(The snake, I mean.)

I

Tu praeter omnes une de capillatis,
cuniculosae Celtiberiae fili,
Egnati, opaca quem bonum facit barba
et dens Hibera defricatus urina.

Egnatius, quod candidos habet dentes,
renidet usque quaque. ....
nunc Celtiber <es>: Celtiberia in terra,
quod quisque minxit, hoc sibi solet mane
dentem atque russam defricare gingiuam,
ut, quo iste uester expolitior dens est,
hoc te amplius bibisse praedicet loti.

Catullus, XXXVII & XXXIX

II

Et delator es et calumniator,
et fraudator es et negotiator,
et fellator es et lanista. miror
quare non habeas, Vaccera, nummos.

Martial, XI.66

III

Καππαδόκην ποτ᾽ ἔχιδνα κακὴ δάκεν. ἀλλὰ καὶ αὐτή
κάτθανε γευσαμένη αἵματος ἰοβόλου

Demodokos, *EG* III

On a very lifelike statue of a dog

I

The sculptor had
to fasten its feet
to this plinth;
otherwise
it would have
run off.

II

The dog-catcher often stops,
to check its license.

III

Other dogs sniff;
cats bristle warily
as they pass;
casual visitors
reach out
a hand to pet.

IV

Biljoe must be
forcibly restrained
from trying
to come on.

I

εἰ μή μου ποτὶ τᾷδε Μύρων πόδας ἥροσε πέτρᾳ
ἄλλαις ἂν νεμόμαν βουσὶν ὁμοῦ δάμαλις

Antipater, AP IX.720

II

ὧδε Μύρων μ᾽ ἔστησε τὸ βοίδιον οἱ δὲ νομῆες
βάλλουσίν με λίθοις ὡς ἀπολειπόμενον

Demetrius of Bithynia, AP IX. 731

III

ἤπαφε καὶ σὲ μύωπα Μύρων, ὅτι κέντρον ἐρείδεις
πλευραῖς χαλκοχύτοις ἀντιτύποιο βοός.
οὐ νέμεσις δὲ μύωπι τί γὰρ τόσον; εἴ γε καὶ αὐτοὺς
ὀφθαλμοὺς νομέων ἠπερόπευσε Μύρων.

Julian of Egypt, AP IX. 739

IV

ἤν μ᾽ ἐσίδῃ μόσχος, μυκήσεται. ἢν δέ γε ταῦρος
βήσεται. ἢν δὲ νομεύς, εἰς ἀγέλαν ἐλάσει

Demetrius of Bithynia, AP IX.730

Neither

The grammarian's daughter was brought to bed
of a gender-balanced set of triplets:
one masculine, one feminine, and Biljoe.

Diuinus

Whenever Carlo complains
of a pain in his 'groin',
Biljoe's laid up with haemorrhoids.
I suppose, it doesn't take a genius
to figure out what those two are up to.

An insult

Accused of murder, air-piracy, assault
with intent to cause grievous bodily harm,
armed robbery, solecism, walking on the grass,
arson, trafficing in illegal substances,
income-tax evasion, unnatural vice,
creating a public nuisance,conspiracy
to commit terrorist acts, and associating
on friendly terms with a certain Biljoe,
the defendants indignantly denied
the last charge.

Carol again

Carol has an itch;
can't find a man to scratch it.
The reason?

> Obesity? Warts?
> Excessive bodily hair?
> Bad complexion?
> Stretch-marks?
>   Hidden deformities?

Nothing so crude;
her physique may be fine.
It's just: she's a moron.

γραμματικοῦ θυγάτηρ ἔτεκεν φιλότητι μιγεῖσα
παιδίον ἀρσενικόν, θηλυκόν, οὐδέτερον.

Palladas, AP IX. 489

Mentula cum doleat puero, tibi, Naevole, culus,
non sum diuinus, sed scio quid facias.

Martial, III. 71

Vis futui nec uis mecum, Saufeia, lauari.
nescio quod magnum suspicor esse nefas.
aut tibi pannosae dependent pectore mammae
aut sulcos uteri prodere nuda times
aut infinito lacerum patet inguen hiatu
aut aliquid cunni prominet ore tui.
sed nihil est horum, credo, pulcherrima nuda es.
si uerum est, uitium peius habes: fatua es.

Martial III. 72

51

Ariadne

I

Abandoned on the island of Naxos
Ariadne took to drink.

II

His father always had been keen on riddles,
word-games, secret codes. That sort of thing.
Now as they approached the coast,
there was something about the rigging.
If only he could remember.
He also had the nagging sense
he had mislaid something
on one of those islands.

III

As she watched the ship disappear in the
distance, she thought of some
needlework she had left unfinished
in the Palace in Knossos.

IV

How many tricks, she wondered,
would she have to turn
to make it back to Crete.

V

Her first husband, she would say,
had been sweet, but dim.
Very dim. The second,
a charming and flamboyant rogue,
was a bit too devoted
to John Barleycorn. She was happiest
with the third, a local slave-trader
and auctioneer, a reliable, energetic
man, in later days a keen gardener.

Variations on Kallimachos

I

The stranger was laconic:
'Billie Lee Peabody, Savannah, Georgia',
but I realized it was the start
of a long and very boring story.

II

The stranger was laconic:
'Theroides Kakadoupoulou, from Krete'.
How many, I thought, are the gifts
of Hellas to the world.

III

The stranger was laconic:
'Haillie Sellasie, Lion of Judah'
but I was having none of that.

IV

The stranger was laconic:
'I have a bomb'
No one, of course, believed him,
to start.

σύντομος ἦν ὁ ξεῖνος, ὃ καὶ στίχος οὐ μακρὰ λέξων
　'Θῆρις Ἀρισταίου Κρής', ἐπ᾽ ἐμοὶ δολιχός

Kallimachos, *EG* XXXV

Tragedy

And who's a handsome fellow now?
Children have decked you out
in splendid finery, put reins
and a bridle on you,
and taught you to race,
like a horse, round the temple,
so that the god can watch
and laugh. And don't you look
the smartest goat *ever*.
After this round of dance
we'll go to the altar.

Inscription on a tomb

Parmis
a fisherman,
choked on a fish
he had just caught.
Monument erected by his
friend and fellow-fisher F. Fisher.

Medeia

Stone from stone
empty now it falls
useless as a word
and then the fire comes,
but on which side?

Twice she endured it,
yellow to red
and back again;
the blaze of light
– o wonder! –
a fence to keep away
their hate, a car.

ἡνία δή τοι παῖδες ἐπί, τράγε, φοινικόεντα
θέντες καὶ λασίῳ φιμὰ περὶ στόματι
ἵππια παιδεύουσι θεοῦ περὶ ναὸν ἄεθλα
ὄφρ᾽ αὐτοὺς ἐφορῇ νήπια τερπομένους

Anyte, EG XIII

Πάρμις ὁ Καλλιγνώτου ἐπακταῖος καλαμευτής
ἄκρος καὶ κίχλης καὶ σκάρου ἰχθυβολεύς
καὶ λάβρου πέρκης δελεάρπαγος, ὅσσα τε κοίλας
σήραγγας πέτρας τ᾽ ἐμβυθίους νέμεται,
ἄγρης ἐκ πρώτης ποτ᾽ ἰουλίδα πετρήεσσαν
δακνάζων ὀλοὴν ἐξ ἁλὸς ἀράμενος
ἔφθιτ᾽. ὀλισθηρὴ γὰρ ὑπὲκ χερὸς ἀίξασα
ᾤχετ᾽ ἐπὶ στεινὸν παλλομένη φάρυγα.
χὠ μὲν μηρίνθων καὶ δούνακος ἀγκίστρων τε
ἐγγὺς ἀπὸ πνοιὴν ἧκε κυλινδόμενος,
νήματ᾽ ἀναπλήσας ἐπιμοίρια. τοῦ δὲ θανόντος
Γρίπων ὁ γριπεὺς τοῦτον ἔχωσε τάφον.

Leonidas of Tarentum, EG LXVI

τοιόνδ᾽ ὄχημα πατρὸς Ἥλιος πατὴρ
δίδωσιν ἡμῖν, ἔρυμα πολεμίας χερός.

Euripides, Medeia 1321-2

Kunoskephalai

I

Without funeral rites and without proper burial,
passer-by, on this mound in Thessaly we lie,
all 30 000 of us; bad news for Macedon.
That cockiness of Philipp's
has vanished quick as a rabbit.

(Alkaios)

II

Without bark and without leaves,
passer-by, on this hill is fixed
a sharpened stake,
waiting patiently for Alkaios.

(Philipp)

Leo mansuetus

What good did it do you
to unlearn violence,
to hold back and perform tricks?
Now you're trampled to death
by a tame menagerie.

I

ἄκλαυστοι καὶ ἄθαπτοι, ὁδοιπόρε, τῷδ᾿ ἐπὶ τύμβῳ
Θεσσαλίας τρισσαὶ κείμεθα μυριάδες,
Ἠμαθίᾳ μέγα πῆμα. τὸ δὲ θρασὺ κεῖνο Φιλίππου
πνεῦμα θοῶν ἐλάφων ᾤχετ᾿ ἐλαφρότερον.

Alkaios, *EG* IV

II

ἄφλοιος καὶ ἄφυλλος, ὁδοιπόρε, τῷδ᾿ ἐπὶ νώτῳ
Ἀλκαίῳ σταυρὸς πήγνυται ἡλιβάτος.

Philipp of Macedon, *EG*

Quid tibi monstrata mansuescere profuit ira?
quid scelus humanasque animo dediscere caedes
imperiumque pati et domino parere minori?
quid, quod abire domo rursusque in claustra reuerte
suetus et a capta iam sponte recedere praeda
insertasque manus laxo dimittere morsu?
occidis, altarum uastator docte ferarum,
non grege Massylo curuaque indagine clausus,
sed uictus fugiente fera.

Statius, Silvae II.5

Crux

Diophon, seeing another crucified near him
on a higher cross than his, felt very bad.
The moral: Eschew envy,
a most uncomfortable sentiment.

Sappho's view

Dying is no fun.
At least the gods don't think so.
Won't catch them dying.

Olé

Everything is a joke;
everything is dust.
Todos esta nada.
Nothing makes any sense
at all. *Olé!*

Greetings

THIS IS THE MAUSOLEUM
OF MARCUS CAECILIUS.
Thanks for the visit, friend.
Be well, and sleep soundly.
One way or the other, I'm sure,
I'll be seeing you again soon.

μακροτέρῳ σταυρῷ σταυρούμενον ἄλλον ἑαυτοῦ
ὁ φθονερὸς Διοφῶν ἔγγυς ἰδὼν ἐτάκη.

Lucillius, *AP* XI. 192

τὸ ἀποθνήσκειν κακόν. οἱ θεοὶ γὰρ οὕτω
κεκρίκασιν. ἀπέθνησκον γὰρ ἄν.

Sappho (quoted by Aristotle *Rhetorica* 1398b 29)

πάντα γέλως, καὶ πάντα κόνις, καὶ πάντα τὸ μηδέν.
πάντα γὰρ ἐξ ἀλόγων ἐστὶ τὰ γίνομενα

Glukon, *AP* X. 124

Hoc est factum monumentum Maarco Caicilio.
Hospes, gratum est quom apud meas restitistei seedes.
bene rem geras et valeas, dormias sine qura.

CIL I.2.1202

59

Copa

Expertly, to the click of her castanets
she arches her flanks. Why exhaust oneself
in the summer heat? They have wine, nuts,
and fruit. The smoke is not from cigarettes.
Tobacco won't be here for another
milennium and a half; otherwise
the scene is familiar.

Sit in the shade; now even the lizards
have found a cool refuge.

Don't water your wine; if she could
speak, you know what death would
whisper, twisting your ear:
'...while you can; I'm coming.'

Prologue

I never washed my face with cool retsina
or kipped beneath a bridge out of the rain.
I never fell asleep inside a bookshop;
I come a semi-pagan to the feast.
Who taught the parrot his cheery *'Ciao!'*?
turned on the tape to imitate our speech?
Who coached the voice of e-mail?
Some silicated PhD (no doubt). One glimpse
of greenbacks, even a mirage, and crows rise
from the trees. What won't they do for art?

Copa Surisca, caput Graeca redimita mitella,
  crispum sub crotalo docta mouere latus,
ebria fumosa saltat lasciua taberna
  ad cubitum raucos excutiens calamos.
quid iuuat aestiuo defessum puluere abisse
  quam potius bibulo decubisse toro?
.....
nunc cantu crebro rumpunt arbusta cicadae,
  nunc uaria in gelida sede lacerta latet:
si sapis, austiuo recubans {nunc} prolue uitro,
seu uis crystalli ferre nouos calices.
.....
quid cineri ingrato seruas bene olentia serta?
  anne coronato uis lapide ossa tegi?
pone merum et talos; pereat qui crastina curat:
  Mors aurem uellens 'uiuite ' ait 'uenio'.

                    Copa (*Appendix Vergiliana*)

Nec fronte labra prolui caballino
nec in bicipiti somniasse Parnaso
memini, ut repente sic poeta prodirem.
Heliconidasque pallidamque Pirenen
illis remitto quorum imagines lambunt
hederae sequaces: ipse semipaganus
ad sacra uatum carmen adfero nostrum.
quis expediuit psittaco suum 'chaere',
picamque docuit uerba nostra conari?
magister artis ingenique largitor
uenter, negatas artifex sequi uoces.
quod si dolosi spes refulserit nummi,
coruos poetas et poetridas picas
cantare credas Pegaseium nectar.

                    Persius, *Prologus*

61

Gallus

A priest of Cybele
wandering in the woods
came on a lion.

He chanted,
beat the sacred tambourine,
held up the pickling jar
in which he kept
the member he'd cut off
to honour the Great Mother.

The lion ran away.

Epicurus

For ages human life lay crushed:
religion forced our faces down
into the mud. A Greek then
was the first who dared
to raise his head up and resist.

Gods

At one time the gods
would appear on earth;
now all we can see
are shapeless wisps
in the sacred precincts
dispersing as quickly
as they begin.

Σάρδις Πεσσινόεντες ἀπὸ Φρυγὸς ἤθελ᾿ ἱκέσθαι,
  ἔκφρων μαινομένην δοὺς ἀνέμοισι τρίχα,
ἁγνὸς ῎Ατυς Κυβέλης θαλαμηπόλος, ἄγρια δ᾿ αὐτοῦ
  ἐψύχθη χαλεπῆς πνεύματα θευφορίης
ἑσπέριον στείχοντος ἀνὰ κνέφας, ἐις δὲ κάταντες
  ἄντρον ἔδυ νεύσας βαιὸν ἄπωθεν ὁδοῦ.
τοῦ δὲ λέων ὤρουσε κατὰ στίβον, ἀνδράσι δεῖμα
  θαρσαλέοις, Γάλλῳ δ᾿ οὐδ᾿ ὀνομαστὸν ἄχος.
ὃς τότ᾿ ἄναυδος ἔμεινε δέους ὕπο, καί τινος αὔρῃ
  δαίμονος ἐς τὸν ἑὸν τύμπανον ἧκε χέρας,
οὗ βαρὺ μυκήσαντος ὁ θαρσαλεώτερος ἄλλων
  τετραπόδων ἐλάφων ἔδραμεν ὀξύτερον,
τὸν βαρὺν οὐ μείνας ἀκοῇ ψόφον. ἐκ δ᾿ εβόησεν·
Μῆτερ, Σαγγαρίου χείλεσι πὰρ ποταμοῦ
ἱρὴν σοὶ θαλάμην ζωάγρια καὶ λαλάγημα
  τοῦτο τὸ θηρὶ φυγῆς αἴτιον ἀντίθεμαι.

Dioscurides, AP VI. 220

Humana ante oculos foede cum uita iaceret
in terris oppressa graui sub religione,
quae caput a caeli regionibus ostendebat
horribili super aspectu mortalibus instans,
primum Graius homo mortalis tollere contra
est oculos ausus primusque obsistere contra.

Lucretius, I.62ff.

γαῖαν μὲν φανέουσι θεοί ποτε, νῦν δὲ πάρεστιν
  αἰψηρῶν ἀνέμων μοῦνον ὁρᾶν τέμενος

Philetas of Kos, EG II

Aster

I

When you peer out at the stars, my Aster, I envy the heavens.
    If I had so many eyes, all of them would look at you.

II

Aster, among the living you shone like the Star of the Morning;
    though extinct you still shine, Evening Star of the dead.

III

Looking up at the stars I know quite well
    that Aster's there and not in hell.

Dion

Tears were marked out
for the women of Troy
from long before their birth,
but for you, Dion,
the future seemed open.
One dead man
is like another;
once though you
drove me wild with desire.

Pilot

The pilot walks along the beach
at the end of the voyage, modestly.
For some on board
it might have been better
if the ship had sunk.

I

ἀστέρας εἰσαθρεῖς, ἀστὴρ ἐμός. εἴθε γενοίμην
οὐρανός, ὡς πολλοῖς ὄμμασιν εἰς σὲ βλέπω.

II

ἀστὴρ πρὶν μὲν ἔλαμπες ἐνὶ ζωοῖσιν ἑῷος,
    νῦν δὲ θανὼν λάμπεις ἕσπερος ἐν φθιμένοις

Plato, *EG* I & II

δάκρυα μὲν Ἑκάβῃ τε καὶ Ἰλιάδεσσι γυναιξί
Μοῖραι ἐπέκλωσαν δὴ τότε γεινομέναις.
σοὶ δέ, Δίων, ῥέξαντι καλῶν ἐπινίκιον ἔργων
δαίμονες εὐρείας ἐλπίδας ἐξέχεαν.
κεῖσαι δ' εὐροχόρῳ ἐν πατρίδι τίμιος ἀστοῖς
    ὦ ἐμὸν ἐκμήνας θυμὸν ἔρωτι Δίων.

Plato, *EG* X

< ὁ δὲ κυβερνήτης > ἐκβὰς παρὰ τὴν θάλλαταν καὶ τὴν ναῦν
περιτατεῖ ἐν μετρίῳ σχήματι. λογίζεσθαι γὰρ οἶμαι ἐπίσταται ὅτι
ἄδηλόν ἐστιν οὕστινας τε ὠφέληκεν τῶν συμπλεόντων οὐκ ἐάσας
καταποντωθῆναι καὶ οὕστινας ἔβλαψεν

Plato, *Gorgias* 511e

65

Fortuna

If we all watched
what we're about,
fortune would lose
her nimbus.
What power she has
she has from us.

Epitaph of Epictetus

Piss-poor I was,
a slave and a cripple,
but a friend of the gods.

The Epicurean doctrine

No need to fear the gods.
No need to shy away from death.
The good is easy to get;
the dreadful easy to bear.

Animula

You always were a vagrant, soul,
a charming, temporary guest
here in my body.
Where are you off to now,
poor unprotected little friend?
And why for once
have you no jokes to crack?

Nullum numen habes si sit prudentia: nos, te,
nos facimus, Fortuna, deam.

Juvenal X. 365f.

δοῦλος Ἐπίκτητος γενόμην, καὶ σῶμ᾽ ἀνάπηρος,
καὶ πενίην Ἶρος, καὶ φίλος ἀθανάτοις.

Anonymus, *AP* VII. 676

ἄφοβον ὁ θέος
ἀνύποπτον ὁ θάνατος.
τἀγαθὸν μὲν εὔκτητον,
τὸ δὲ δεινὸν εὐεκκαρτέρητον.

Philodemus, *Adversus sophistas* 4.7-14 (ed. Gigante)

Animula uagula blandula
hospes comesque corporis
quae nunc abibis in loca
pallidula, rigida, nudula
nec ut soles dabis iocos?

The Emperor Hadrian

The poet & the politicians

I

The Metelli consuls? Our bad luck.
We Romans just have to put up with it.
(Naevius)

II

The Metelli inform Naevius the poet
they intend to hurt him where he'll feel it.
(Q. Caecilius Metellus)

The poet's epitaph on himself

If gods may mourn men,
me they'll mourn,
for since I was sent
into storage here
the Romans have lost
the Latin language.

Bucolic

Covered with snow
the cows came home
at dusk by themselves.
Therimachos is still asleep
out there under the oak,
where the lightning struck.

I

Fato Metelli Romae fiunt consules

II

Malum dabunt Metelli Naeuio poetae

Naevius 47/46, (ed. Diehl, Bonn 1911)

Immortales mortales si foret fas flere
flerent diuae Camenae Naeuium poetam.
itaque, postquam est Orchi traditus thesauro
obliti sunt Romae loquier lingua latina.

Naevius (ed. Diehl, Bonn 1911)

αὐτόμαται δείλῃ ποτὶ ταὔλιον αἱ βόες ἦλθον
ἐξ ὄρεος πολλῇ νειφόμεναι χιόνι.
αἰαῖ Θηρίμαχος δὲ παρὰ δρυῒ τὸν μακρὸν εὕδει
ὕπνον. ἐκοιμήθη δ' ἐκ πυρὸς οὐρανίου.

Diotimos, *EG* X

Kleis

I don't know where
I could get you a ribbon
for your hair, Kleis.
They are established
in Mytilene. We lost.

Μεταβολή

Hector, tell Achilles
the Myrmidons are all dead
and Thessaly lies under the heel
of the sons of Aeneas.

Cato

On the winning side
the gods smile,
but Cato still
prefers the other.

σοὶ δ᾽ ἔγω Κλέι ποικίλαν
οὐκ ἔχω πόθεν ἔσσεται
μιτράν <αν> ἀλλὰ τῶι Μυτιληνάωι
....
παι.α.ειον εχην πο./
αικε.η ποικιλασκ..../
ταῦτα τὰς Κλεανακτίδα /
φύγας /

Sappho, LG 219

Ἕκτορ, Ἀρήιον αἷμα, κατὰ χθονὸς εἴ που ἀκούεις,
  χαῖρε καὶ ἄμπνευσον βαιὸν ὑπὲρ πατρίδος.
Ἴλιον οἰκεῖται, κλεινὴ πόλις, ἄνδρας ἔχουσα
  σοῦ μὲν ἀφαυροτέρους ἀλλ᾽ ἔτ᾽ ἀπηϊφίλος,
Μυρμιδόνες δ᾽ ἀπόλοντο. παρίστασο καὶ λέγ᾽ Ἀχιλλεῖ
  Θεσσαλίην κεῖσθαι πᾶσαν ὑπ᾽ Αἰνεάδαις.

The Emperor Tiberius

Martia progenies, Hector, tellure sub ima,
  fas audire tamen si mea uerba tibi,
respira, quoniam uindex tibi contigit heres,
  qui patriae famam proferat usque tuae.
Ilios en surgit rursum inclita, gens colit illam
  te Marte inferior, Martis amica tamen,
Mymonidas periisse omnes dic, Hector Achilli,
  Thessaliam et magnis esse sub Aeneadis.

Germanicus Caesar

Victrix causa deis placuit, sed uicta Catoni

Lucan, I.135

Achilles to Patroklos

I wish to god they'd all die:
Trojans, Greeks. Not one
escape, not one,
and you and I,
the two of us alone,
survive to strip Troy
bare and pluck her jewel

Dominus et deus

I, Imperator Domitianus Caesar
Augustus Germanicus Dacicus,
give you a monthly dole of corn,
triumphs over our enemies,
magnificent public buildings,
and now a mock sea-battle
in the flooded arena;
you give me a *book*?
You and your book, I think,
are itching for a drenching.

Myth comes alive!

That criminal must have been
a dreadful fellow, a temple-robber,
arsonist, perhaps a slave who murdered
his own master, something like that,
but Caesar in his wisdom has found out
a useful role for him, too, as protagonist
in this vivid performance
of '*The Crucifixion of Laurenteolus*'.

αἲ γάρ, Ζεῦ τε πάτερ καὶ Ἀθηναίη καὶ ᾽Απολλον,
μήτε τις οὖν Τρώων θάνατον φύγοι ὅσσοι ἔασι
μήτε τις ᾽Αργείων, νῶϊν δ᾽ ἐκδῦμεν ὄλεθρον
ὄφρ᾽ οἶοι Τροίης ἱερὰ κρήδεμνα λύωμεν.

Iliad XVI.97ff.

Do tibi naumachiam, tu das epigrammata nobis:
uis, puto, cum libro, Marce, natare tuo.

Martial, I. 5

Qualiter in Scythica religatus rupe Prometheus
*   assiduam nimio pectore pauit auem,*
nuda Caledonio sic uiscera praebuit urso
*   non falsa pendens in cruce Laureolus.*
uiuebant laceri membris stillantibus artus
*   inque omni nusquam corpore corpus erat.*
denique supplicium <dignus tulit: ille parentis>
*   uel domini iugulum foderat ense nocens,*
templa uel arcano demens spoliauerat auro,
*   subdiderat saeuas uel tibi, Roma, faces.*
uicerat antiquae sceleratus crimina famae,
*   in quo, quae fuerat fabula, poena fuit.*

Martial, *Lib. spect.* 7

An early form of Kantianism

You think, Hyllus, because you're under age
you can fuck the Police-Chief's wife with impunity.
After all, what could he do,
apart, of course, from sodomizing you a bit?
Cut off your balls, that's what.
Don't tell me he's 'not s'ppozed' to do that.
Are you doing what you're s'ppozed to?

Pyrrho

When the skeptic's wooden shack caught fire,
his neighbours yelled: *'Come out'*.
Standing at the window he replied
that every story had two sides,
although it *seemed* unseasonably
warm... The collapse of the roof
put an end to the debate.

Socrates

Socrates taught anyone,
provided they were 'good'
(right social class,
attractive, young).
He made no distinctions;
like a chalk line drawn
on a white-washed board,
no way to tell whom he preferred.
He had the hots for them all.

Vxorem armati futuis, puer Hylle, tribuni,
  supplicium tantum dum puerile times.
uae tibi, dum ludis, castrabere. iam mihi dices
  'non licet, hoc.' quid? tu quod facis, Hylle, licet?

Martial II.60

– κάτθανες, ὦ Πύρρων; – ἐπέχω. – πυμάτην μετὰ μοῖραν
  φὴς ἐπέχειν; – ἐπέχω. – σκέψιν ἔπαυσε τάφος.

Julian of Egypt, *AP*.VII.576

et amabat omnes; nam ut discrimen non facit
neque signat linea alba

sic Socrates in amore et in adulescentulis
meliore paulo facie; signat nil quem amet.

Quid? Quas partiret ipse <pro> doctrinas bonis...

Lucilius 830-834 (ed. Krenkel, Leiden, 1970)

Imitatio Christi *(modo modo)*

The LORD said: 'Feed My Sheep';
the archbishop fleeces them.

{*ossia:*
Bartholomew (the Disciple)
was skinned alive for the faith;
Bartholomew (the Bishop)
skins the faithful alive.}

Too ugly to serve

In times of trouble, Mark,
the gods demand a human sacrifice.
Don't worry though, you're safe.
They've specified: 'unblemished victim'.

The end

Whoa, little book, that's enough now;
the ink-jet is empty, but you charge on,
out of control. Something, you think,
left unsaid? Whatever it was,
page one already finished it off.
The reader is restive and yawns:
enough is enough.

Tὸ δέον

Two blinded camels grinding corn,
lashed to one pole, they struggle
to coordinate their splay-foot,
ritual gait, and speak of Kant.

In Dominum Bartholemeum Aueroldum,
Episcopum Spalatensem

Aspice dissimiles quam sint duo Bartholomei:
hic pellem Christo sustulit, ille dedit.

Marcus Marulus Spalatensis, 17

Longa, Sabelle, tuo dependet stiria naso:
non possum nasum ferre, Sabelle, tuum!
et pituita subest nigrae foedissima linguae:
non possum linguam ferre, Sabelle, tuam!
emunctae naris sanusque, Sabelle, palato
cum fueris, superis sacrificabo deis.

Marcus Marulus Spalatensis, 11

Ohe, iam satis est, ohe, libelle,
iam peruenimus usque ad umbilicos.
tu procedere adhuc et ire quaeris,
nec summa potes in schida teneri,
sic tamquam tibi res peracta non sit,
quae prima quoque pagina peracta est.
iam lector queriturque deficitque,
iam librarius hoc et ipse dicit
'ohe, iam satis est, ohe, libelle'

Martial, IV. 89

77

Notes

Page 10, Mercenaries:
'*Shqiptar*' (pronounced, roughly 'Shiptar') is Albanian for '(an) Albanian'

Page 12, A.D.14:
The *Res gestae diui Augusti* is an official record of his achievements which the Emperor Augustus had inscribed and publicly displayed in various places. There is a convenient bi-lingual edition (with introduction and commentary) by P.A. Brunt and J.M. Moore (Oxford University Press 1967)

Page 20, A father's wisdom:
Cf. also Norbert Elias *Über den Prozeß der Zivilisation* (Frankfurt/M: Suhrkamp, 1981, two volumes), esp. the section '*Über das Verhalten beim Essen*' pp. 110-174.

Page 24, Illusions:
The Herakleitos mentioned is obviously not identical with the late 7th/early 6th century philosopher from Ephesos.

Page 28, Glubit and *Lost lines from Aeneid VI*:
The exact meaning of the word Catullus uses to describe Lesbia's activity ('*glubit*') is unclear. In other contexts the verb is used to refer to skinning sheep or stripping the bark off trees. '*Glupsitne*' is the third person singular perfect-tense interrogative form of the same verb.

Page 34, More epitaphs II:
Around 279 BC a horde of Celtic tribesmen from the Balkans accepted an invitation from Nikomedes of Bithynia to serve him as mercenaries. In 277/276 BC they plundered the sanctuary of Apollo in Didyma near Miletus. They eventually settled in Asia Minor and became known as the 'Galatians'

Page 37, Scholastikos:
'Scholastikos' ('The Scholar') is a stock figure of humour for his simple-mindedness. A large number of jokes about him (of varying quality) can be found in the ancient joke-book *Philogelos* which is available in a bi-lingual (Greek/German) edition, edited by A. Thierfelder (Munich 1968).

*Page 40, **Apophoreta:***
An *'Apophoreton'* is a gift to be taken home (i.e. 'carried away') by
the guests who are invited to dinner

*Page 42, **On a statue of Priapus:***
This poem was written in early 1997 and contains some slightly dated
historical references. 'Mother Theresa' was an Albanian nun who
had a fascination with death, suffering, and the process of dying
itself, glorifying them as paths to spiritual enlightenment. History
has rendered what was originally a merely indirect allusion to
necrophilia explicit in that Theresa died in late 1997. The 'Spice
Girls' were a group of four or five young female singers who were
popular in the mid-1990s. The 'Pope' is the *'pontifex maximus'* of a
mystery religion which is centred in Rome. The *'Pentateuch'*
recounts the alleged exploits of the itinerant Egyptian priest and
miracle worker 'Moses'.

*Page 42, **Adonis in hell:***
Because of this poem 'Praxilla's Adonis' became a byword for
silliness in the ancient world.

*Page 46, **Biljoe I:***
Several other ancient authors mention this Iberian form of hygiene.

*Page 56, **Kunoskephalai:***
Philipp lost a decisive battle against Roman forces under T.Quinctius
Flaminius at Kunoskephalai (in Thessaly) in 197 BC.

*Page 62, **Gallus:***
Entry into the order of *'galli'* (priests of Cybele, the 'Great Mother')
was restricted to those who had proved their devotion to her by
castrating themselves. The lion is sacred to Cybele. The Greek
version printed here is only one of several variants surviving in *AP*,
and attributed respectively to 'Simonides' (*AP* VI.217), 'Alkaios'
(*AP* VI.218), and 'Antipater' (*AP* VI.219)

*Page 62, **Epicurus:***
Epicurus (*c.* 340-270BC) was an Athenian philosopher who was
famous for his view that the gods, if they existed at all, regarded the
world in which we live with indifference. His main motivation for
this seems to have been an attempt to rid people of fear of death and
of superstitious beliefs about posthumous punishment for wrong-
doing.

*Page 64, **Aster:***
Aster's name means 'star' in Greek; he was said to have died young.

*Page 64, **Dion:***
Dion (409-354 BC) was son-in-law of Dionysios I, tyrant of Syracuse. He enlisted Plato's help in trying to train Dionysios II, son of Dionysios I, to be a philosopher-king. This was a complete failure; the younger Dionysios is said to have been put off by Plato's relentless emphasis on mathematics, preferring alcohol to geometry. After an extremely lengthy and convoluted series of political and military manoeuvres, Dion became tyrant in Syracuse, but was killed by some of his mercenaries, instigated by a man named Kallipos, who was a close associate of Plato's Academy.

*Page 66, **Epitaph of Epictetus:***
Epictetus (*c.* 55-*c.* 135 AD) was a Stoic philosopher who was originally a slave. His master is said to have crippled him unintentionally by twisting his leg too far as punishment for some minor offense.

*Page 66, **Animula:***
The Emperor Hadrian is said to have composed this poem of his death-bed.

*Page 68, **The poet and the politicians:***
The Metelli were an extremely powerful clan, several of whose members reached the consulship during the Republican period. Q. Caecilius Metellus was consul in 206 (BC).

*Page 70, **Kleis:***
Sappho's party lost out to a rival in a power struggle for control of Mitylene, the main city on the island of Lesbos; in exile she is addressing her daughter Kleis.

Page 70 μεταβολή:
Educated Romans of the Imperiod period liked to imagine that they were the descendants of the Trojan hero Aeneas, and thus that Roman hegemony over Greece could be seen as a kind of 'reversal' of the outcome of the Trojan War. D.L. Page argues in *Further Greek Epigrams* (Cambridge University Press 1981, p. 559) that the original version of this poem is the Greek one included in *AP* (IX.387), that it was written by Tiberius, and that the Latin translation is by Tiberius' adopted son Germanicus. Text follows Page.

Page 72, **Dominus et deus:**
Martial assiduously sought the patronage of the Emperor Domitian
(born 51AD, became Emperor 81AD, died 96 AD). Domitian
represents a new stage in the transformation of the Roman polity
from a structure in which at least some of the pieties and external
trappings of republican rule were maintained, if only as a facade,
into the explicitly autocratic rule of a god-king. Earlier Emperors had
been called *'Imperator'* and *'Princeps Senatus'* (*'Commander'*
and *'First Man in the Senate'*); Domitian insisted upon being
addressed as *'Dominus et deus'* (*'Master and God'*).

Page 72, **Myth comes alive!**
Criminals were occasionally executed in the arena in this way. *'The
Crucifixion of Laurenteolus'* was a popular mime about a robber who
is crucified and left on the cross to be torn apart by wild beasts.

Page 76, τὸ δέον:
'τὸ δέον' means roughly 'what ought to be done'.

Biographies

*For further information the reader may usefully consult **Der kleine Pauly** (Deutscher Taschenbuch Verlag, 1979; 5 volumes) or, failing that, **The Oxford Classical Dictionary**.*

Aeschylus
Fifth century (BC) Athenian dramatist.

Alkaios
Poet from Messene (Sicily) who flourished about 200BC. He is not identical with the rather better known Lesbian poet of the same name (*c.* 600BC) who is credited with the invention of 'Alcaic' strophe, a form that has been widely used in ancient and modern times (e.g. by Horace in Latin and Hölderlin in German).

Anthologia Palatina
Name for a collection of ancient epigrams called *'Palatina'* because the manuscript was at one point kept in the *'Bibliotheca Palatina'* in Heidelberg. (Abbreviated *'AP'*).

Antipater of Sidon
Phoenician epigrammatist from the end of the 2nd century (BC) whose work is known through *AP*.

Anyte
From Tegea in the Peleponnese *c.* 300BC; about 20 of her epigrams survive in *AP*.

Archilochos
Earliest Greek lyric poet (7th century BC) of whom any considerable fragments are extant. His poetry described his life as a mercenary soldier, a failed attempt to colonize the island of Thasos, his unhappy love of a young girl named Neoboule, etc. He had a particularly fine line in invective.

Ariston
Known only through epigrams in *AP*.

Bion

Bucolic poet who lived toward the end of the 2nd century.

Carmina anacreonta

The real Anacreon was a sixth century (BC) poet from Teos. His poems came to be seen as the work of a dipso- and eroto-maniac old man. Gradually songs written by various unknown persons in this persona were attributed to 'Anacreon' and eventually collected together with some genuine works by the real Anacreon.

Catullus (C. Valerius Catullus)

Roma poet, born near modern Verona in the late Republican period, probably died in the 50s (BC).

Claudius Claudianus

Last major pagan poet in Rome. Born in Alexandria some time before 400 AD, he wrote first in Greek, then, after moving to Rome (*c.* 395AD), in Latin.

Damocharis

Grammarian from the island of Kos who lived in the 6th century AD.

Demodokos

Poet from Leros, a small island off the coast of Asia Minor who may have flourished *c.* 600 (BC).

Demetrius of Bithynia

Sometimes identified with a Stoic philosopher mentioned in Diogenes Laertius (5.84) but this attribution is speculative.

Dionysios

In the manuscripts the author is called 'Dionysios the Sophist' but nothing else is know about him.

Dioscurides

Lived in the second half of the third century BC in Alexandria.

Diotimos

There were several poets of this name; nothing of interest is known about any of them.

Euripides
> 5th century (BC) Athenian dramatist.

Germanicus Caesar (Nero Claudius Germanicus)
> Born 15 BC, adopted by the Emperor Tiberius 4 AD, died 19 AD. The Emperor Claudius is his brother; the Emperor Gaius his son.

Glukon
> Otherwise unknown poet of some epigrams in *AP*.

Hadrian
> Born 76AD, became Emperor on the death of Trajan (117AD); died 138AD

Julian of Egypt
> Sixth century AD; what we know are his epigrams in *AP*.

Juvenal (D. Iunius Iuuenalis)
> Roman satirist born 67AD in Campania.

Kallimachos
> Early third century (BC) Alexandrian librarian, proto-philologist, and belletrist. Coiner of the famous librarian's motto 'Big book = big pain-in-the-neck' (μέγα βίβλιον μέγα κακόν).

Killaktor
> Otherwise unknown writer to whom some epigrams in *AP* are attributed

Leonidas of Tarentum
> Born in Greek-speaking Southern Italy probably in the early third century BC

Lucan (M. Annaeus Lucanus)
> born 39 AD in Cordova, committed suicide on Nero's orders 65AD; author of an unfinished epic on the wars between Julius Caesar and his 'republican' opponents which is variously called *'Bellum civile'* or *'Pharsalia'*.

Lucilius
> Early Roman satirist who flourished in the second century BC.

Lucillius
> Hellenistic poet of first century AD represented by some epigrams in the *AP*.

Lucretius

Author of an epic poem which gives an exposition of the Epicurean philosophy. Nothing certain is known about his life save that he lived in the late Republican period (97?-55? BC).

Marcus Marulus Spalatensis

The latinized name of the Dalmatian humanist Marko Marulic of Split (1450-1524). Recently a collection of his epigrams has been rediscovered in the University Library Glasgow (*Hunter 334*). The text of this collection in an edition by Darko Novakovic has been published in *Colloquia Maruliana VI* (ed. B. Lucin and M. Tomasovic, *Knjizevski Krug*, Split, 1997).

Martial (M. Valerius Martialis)

Born in Bilbilis (Spain) in about 40 AD. Despite assiduous courting of the Emperor Domitian he had only a moderately successful (in his own eyes a very unsuccessful) literary career in Rome, at the end of which he returned to Spain to die (in about 103/4 AD).

Naeuius

Born in Campania in the third century BC.

Nikarchos

Apparently there were two poets of this name whose work is transmitted in *AP* but nothing of substance is known about either of them.

Nossis

Tells us in one of her epigrams that she is the daughter of a certain Theophilis of Epizephyrian Lokris (Greek-speaking Southern Italy); lived at the beginning of the third century (BC).

Palladas

Alexandrian epigrammatist of the second half of the 4th century AD.

Persius (Aules Persius Flaccus)

Roman satirist born 34 AD in Volterra, died 62AD.

Philetas of Kos

Poet of the late 4th century (BC).

Philodemos
Epicurean philosopher of first century BC originally from Gadara. Papyrus fragments of several of his philosophical works were rediscovered in the 19th century in Herculaneum. Some poems are attributed to him in *AP*.

Philipp of Macedon
The one in question is Philipp V, King of Macedon 221-179 BC, not the father of Alexander the Great.

Plato
Several epigrams are attributed to the 4th century (BC) Athenian philosopher

Praxilla
Born on island of Sikyon in early 5th century (BC); she was credited with the invention of the so-called '*metrum praxilleum*'.

Sappho
Born in late 7th century BC on island of Lesbos.

Statius (P. Papinius Statius)
Born about 40 AD in Naples; author in epic and lyric forms.

Sulpicia
The manuscripts of the works of the first century (BC) Roman poet Tibullus contain some poems that seem not to be by him. They have been attributed to a certain Sulpicia, niece of M. Valerius Messalla Corvinus (also first century BC).

Theokritos
Sicilian bucolic poet of the 3rd century (BC).

Theophrastus
4th century (BC) philosopher who was successor of Aristotle as head of the peripatetic school.

Tiberius (Tiberius Claudius Nero)
Born 42 BC, adopted by the Emperor Augustus 4 AD. On Augustus' death in 14AD, succeeded him as '*Princeps*' (= de facto 'Emperor'); died 37 AD.

Tymnes
Known only from a handful of epigrams in *AP*

For a complete list of Hearing Eye publications, please write enclosing an SAE to:

Hearing Eye, Box 1, 99 Torriano Avenue, London NW5 2RX